Incident Names

New Women's Voices Series, No. 189

poems by

S.J. Pearce

Finishing Line Press
Georgetown, Kentucky

Incident Names

ACKNOWLEDGMENTS

"A Discalced Queen…" was first published under the title "Penelopiad" in
The Plenitudes Journal: https://www.theplentitudes.com/piece/penelopiad
"The Best of Your Parts…" was first published under the title "Trigger
Warning" in *The Reform Jewish Quarterly*
"Psalm 144: Crusader" was first published in *River Heron Review* (October
2022): *https://www.riverheronreview.com/sj-pearce*; it was subsequently
nominated for Best of the Net
"Meeting Three Ghosts in Belchite la Vieja" was first published in *The Laurel
Review*
"Someday, Underwater Archaeologists," was first published in *Frontier
Poetry*: *https://www.frontierpoetry.com/2024/02/09/sj-pearce*
"Tiraz" and "Ars Poetica" were finalists for the 2024 *Tupelo Quarterly*
Poetry Prize: *https://www.tupeloquarterly.com/poetry/sj-pearce-couplet-with-
federico-garcia-lorcas-ode-to-walt-whitman-tiraz/*

Publisher: Leah Huete de Maines
Editor: Christen Kincaid
Cover Art: S.J. Pearce
Author Photo: Liesa Thompson
Cover Design: Elizabeth Maines McCleavy

Order online: www.finishinglinepress.com
also available on amazon.com

Author inquiries and mail orders:
Finishing Line Press
PO Box 1626
Georgetown, Kentucky 40324
USA

Contents

The Department of Lost Books
Ars Poetica after Joe Brainard

I remember trying to be left-handed.

I remember being stuck with a really goofy-looking signature on my green plastic library card until I was eighteen because of it.

I remember when library fines weren't enforced for under-eighteens in San Francisco.

I remember getting to college believing that due dates were just suggested times when the library thought it would be nice to have the book back.

I remember racking up hundreds of dollars of fines that way.

I remember my parents paying. (They remember, too.)

I remember the altar in the cathedral of knowledge.

I remember the high tables and the card catalogues before they were removed to make space for newer technologies.

I remember being in Jerusalem that year, wasting away a bit, and unable to go and to claim one of those tables where I had spent so many hours learning Arabic just a few years before, where Julia Roberts sat in *Mona Lisa Smile*.

I remember doing a little butt-dance in the movie theater seat when I saw that scene.

I remember going much later to the Elmer Holmes Bobst library— which looks like the supernova created when the state penitentiary careened into an unsuspecting game of Tetris—embarrassed over a $34 fine.

I remember the librarian at the circulation desk telling me that if the fine wasn't into four figures, there was nothing to be embarrassed about.

I remember wondering what NYU students do with their library books.

I remember before the static, metal, Tetris-game screen went up around the atrium to prevent suicides from the top floor.

I remember when the San Francisco Public Library opened the new main building with such a gaping-soaring atrium that they had to send most of the books to storage, where they got wet and moldy.

I remember choosing never to go back once the bathroom became a shooting gallery.

I remember seeing the main branch a few years later on season thirteen of Top Chef.

I remember being happy that research librarians were getting a shout-out but confused about what the "Viking cuisine" was that the chefs were getting help researching.

I remember quietly talking my way into the Biblioteca Nacional de España as an undergraduate.

I remember the security guards asking me why I was standing so far away from them.

I remember being allowed to bring cigarettes and a lighter into the reading room but not earphones.

I remember the short-haired civil-servant security guard who searched my pencil pouch—"for scissors," she said—when I exited, as if I might have cut pages out of the rare books, as if it wouldn't have been too late.

I remember the guy who was smarter than scissors and built an underworld empire selling rare maps cut out of libraries' rare books with cotton floss moistened inside his cheek.

I remember seeing that same guard a few years later after she got a promotion within the Ministry of Culture to the door of the gallery with the Lichtensteins at the Queen Sofia Museum of Modern Art.

I remember that everyone still called her the dragon-lady guard.

I remember the chintz in the Andrew D. White Library and the soaring view out the picture windows behind the velvet armchairs.

I remember the friend who got married there and didn't invite me.

I remember the Cornell students who had better places to kill themselves than in the library.

I remember my own student who died in a car crash in Ithaca his senior year.

I remember starting off the next class session in a basement room by suggesting we dedicate our day of learning to his memory.

I remember wondering if I had just given away that I am Jewish with that rhetorical move.

I remember I wasn't always so macabre. (That's a lie.)

I remember that the Latin word for left-handed is something like sinister.

I remember being charmed by the video of Doug Emhoff visiting the Library of Congress.

I remember pissing off the Judaica librarian there.

I remember the American archive in Jerusalem that built new shelving straight across a closet door but forgot to empty out the closet first.

I remember my certainty that the documents I needed were in that closet.

I remember reading *The Purloined Letter* and *The Cask of Amontillado* in Mrs. Hernández's 9th grade honors English class.

I remember that other archive, in the basement of a poet's house-museum in Tel Aviv, that only opens at 6pm on two Mondays a month when the museum is closed.

I remember working through the night because that's when the archivist works.

I remember my deep relief that his personal idiosyncrasies are professional, limited to the hours he keeps and his sense of ownership over the collection.

I remember planning the ways I might hop the fence to get in.

I remember planning the ways I might hop the fence to get out.

I remember the fresh-squeezed orange juice we drank when we took a break at 11pm.

I remember my then-boyfriend taking me to the British Library.

I remember he made sure I understood what the desk attendant with the thick Windrush accent had said to me.

I remember that too many years later he would go on to vote for Brexit and ask me if he had hurt me.

I remember that he did not like my answer.

I remember when I learned to stop asking questions I did not want answered.

I remember renewing my library card ahead of time.

I remember signing neatly, with my right hand.

Tiraz[1]

"The truth is, the Viking textile from Birka has no Arabic on it at all."
—Stephennie Mulder, "The Rise and Fall of the 'Viking Allah' Textile,"
https://hyperallergic.com/407746/refuting-viking-allah-textiles-meaning/

"For brevity's sake, we may call [this] 'tall-short-tall syndrome.'"
—Richard Ettinghausen, "Kufesque in Byzantine Greece, the Latin West,
and the Muslim World."

1.

لـاﺟلـاﺟلـاﺟلـاﺟلـاﺟلـاﺟلـاﺟلـاﺟلـاﺟلـاﺟلـاﺟلـاﺟلـاﺟلـاﺟلـاﺟلـاﺟلـاﺟلـاﺟلـاﺟلـا

And maybe it means health and happiness. Abbreviated, naturally.

لـاﺟلـاﺟلـاﺟلـاﺟلـاﺟلـاﺟلـاﺟلـاﺟلـاﺟلـاﺟلـاﺟلـاﺟلـاﺟلـاﺟلـاﺟلـاﺟلـاﺟلـاﺟلـاﺟلـا

Hold it up to a mirror, let it reflect what you wish to read.

لـاﺟلـاﺟلـاﺟلـاﺟلـاﺟلـاﺟلـاﺟلـاﺟلـاﺟلـاﺟلـاﺟلـاﺟلـاﺟلـاﺟلـاﺟلـاﺟلـاﺟلـاﺟلـاﺟلـا

Maybe it is proof of Vikings. And maybe it is the name of God.

لـاﺟلـاﺟلـاﺟلـاﺟلـاﺟلـاﺟلـاﺟلـاﺟلـاﺟلـاﺟلـاﺟلـاﺟلـاﺟلـاﺟلـاﺟلـاﺟلـاﺟلـاﺟلـاﺟلـا

And maybe the name of God is proof of Vikings.

لـاﺟلـاﺟلـاﺟلـاﺟلـاﺟلـاﺟلـاﺟلـاﺟلـاﺟلـاﺟلـاﺟلـاﺟلـاﺟلـاﺟلـاﺟلـاﺟلـاﺟلـاﺟلـاﺟلـا

2.

بسم الله الرحمن الرحيم : بركة كاملة بركة كاملة بركة كاملة بركة كاملة
نصر من الله لعبد ابي تميم الامام المستنصر بالله امير المؤمنين

Illegible.

---

[1]"Ṭirāz (plural ṭuruz): Embroidery or decorative work on a garment or piece of fabric. It later came to mean a robe of honour, richly adorned with elaborate embroidery, especially in the form of embroidered bands with writing upon them. In the earliest centuries of Islam, such a garment was worn by rulers and members of their entourage. A secondary development from the meaning 'embroidered strip of writing' is that of 'strip of writing,' border or braid in general, applied not only to inscriptions woven, embroidered, or sewn on materials, but also to any inscriptions on a band of any kind, whether hewn out of stone, done in mosaic, glass or faience, or carved in wood" (*Encyclopaedia of Islam*, 2nd ed.).

The Best of Your Parts is Your Greatest Lie

A palinode against The Touchstone by Qalonymos ben Qalonymos[2]

You are a poet and the best of your parts is your greatest lie.
You are, as the kids say, punching down.
You have convinced them you are not.
You got them to believe you are on their side. You are not.
You are sincere? You are a cynic. You are sarcastic.
You: the nominative and the accusative. You name and I accuse.
You: a social, grammatical man. You are a palindrome because
you are the son of your father.
You demur. You know how lucky you are each morning to say: *Blessed are*
You, o Lord, our God, who did not make me a woman, who did not
make me a slave, who did not make me one of them.

You say you long to be like Dinah. No one longs to be like Dinah.
You know what women are.
You do not wish to pray to a God who made you flawed but according to His will.
You cannot stay mum about your fortune to those of us He did make women.
You deign. You debase. You condescend.

You list the minor benefits of our lesser condition as if we won't notice what we are missing. You are dead. You are open to interpretation. You might be surprised. You are not mine to abjure. But all the same, each morning I say: **Blessed are You, o Lord, my God, who did not make me an earnest reader of satire.**

[2]The best and most accessible English translation of Qalonymos' poem may be found under the title "On Becoming a Woman" in Peter Cole, *The Dream of the Poem*. Princeton: UP, 2007. 285.

A Discalced Queen Waits in the Security Checkpoint Line at the Ithaca-Tompkins International Airport

"So every day she wove the mighty cloth,
and then at night by torchlight, she unwove it...

"We caught her there, unraveling the cloth,
and made her finish it. This is our answer..."

The Odyssey, Book 2.105-6, 2.11-12,
trans. Emily Wilson

Cast on fifteen stitches in tiny yarn:
gauge-one needles, a millimeter thick,
and knit yourself an amulet: a scarf
that you will never finish.

Gauge-one needles, a millimeter thick,
are no threat to aviation security.
But you will never finish;
and through your travels it will protect you.

It's no threat to aviation security,
so take it with you when you go, where you go
and through your travels it will protect you.
Knit, unknit, rip back, keep knitting.

Take it with you when you go, where you go.
You and no agent will do the unknitting.
Knit, unknit, rip back, keep knitting
until you like it better that way.

You and no gent will do the unknitting
at the checkpoint where points are a threat.
You like it better that way.
Slide the stiches off the needles.

At the checkpoint, a point is a threat.
Tension increases and stitches grow smaller.
Slide the stitches off the needles.
What are you doing? Protecting yourself.

Tension increases and stitches grow smaller
It's a stranger sitting next to you who asks
what you are doing. Protecting yourself:
Rip back, keep knitting, don't look up, keep knitting.

It's stranger, sitting next to you,
knitting always along the way.
Rip back, keep knitting, don't look up, keep knitting.
Incomplete, it's always an excuse.

Knitting always along the way, those
short, small, tense, repeating stripes.
Incomplete, there's always an excuse.
Thousands of repeats to surround your neck.

Short, small, tense, repeating stripes
against constricting questions from the middle seat
Thousands of repeats to surround your neck
and dampen the sound of unwelcome conversation.

Constricting questions about the Middle East:
Loops of yarn form *fā', qāf, mīm, wāw*
and dampen the sounds of unwelcomed consonants
in the books that I packed away.

Loops of yarn form *qāf, mīm, wāw, yā'*,
curling up *qawmī*, my nation, hidden
in the books that I packed away,
under an English Bible to deflect.

Qawmī, my nation, hidden:
letters in order, in knitted stripes
under an English Bible to deflect
the x-irradiation of blunt needles and Arabic books

Letters in order, in knitted stripes,
then loops slid off needles and words erased
The ex-irradiation of blunt needles and Arabic books:
dark and light, light and dark.

Then: loops slid off needles and words erased
Now everything, add anger
Light and dark, dark and light.
The stripes stack up until you tear them back again.

Now everything is a danger:
they are real and you imagined.
The stripes stack up until you tear them back again,
protecting yourself from false security.

Ephemeral, and you imagined
fifteen stitches cast on in tiny yarn:
Protect yourself from false security
and knit yourself an amulet that you will never finish.

A Journey in the Present Millennium

Excerpted and redacted from A.B. Yehoshua's Journey to the End of the Millennium, trans. Nicholas de Lange, pursuant to the Code of Federal Regulations, Title 49, Subtitle A, Part 15, "Protection of Sensitive Transportation Security Information"

But will there be anyone to remember

that ancient soul,

the transient shadow of our

internal organs?

Liquids, miniaturized

for travel—

Are   your heroes now

anything at all?

Clear

cavemen

at the

bottom of a forgotten drawer

survive. Or

our image can,   a

twin   to ourselves.

Incident Names

*"A DESCRIPTIVE NAME is one that originates from some permanent
or semi-permanent quality of the place itself. The practical test of a
descriptive name may be said to be that a traveler coming to the place
of naming should be able to recognize the reason for the naming. The
majority of descriptive names perpetuate a quality of the place that can
be appreciated by one of the senses, most commonly sight... INCIDENT
NAMES identify the place by means of some incident which has occurred
at or near it. As opposed to descriptive names, incident names record only
a temporary characteristic or association of the place."*

—*George R. Stewart, "A Classification of Place Names," in Names: A
Journal of Onomastics 2:1 (1954)*

My age is a blue-green field of columbine
in a paddock of bison in Golden Gate Park.
(Call them buffalo and they'll know

you're not from here.) My pulse quickens
walking Baker Beach, crossing the bridge,
my twin from another, less pock-marked era,

to the headlands, park lands, a virgin sequoia grove:
orange bark older than Jesus, gray-green trees of life,
where shawl-ends of fog burn with the aurora.

I hike to the spiral jetty: installation art,
a shell-covered, sandy hook jutting out into the bay.
Old mounds and new are designed and erode.

I take a bus back to the city: transit center,
Moscone center, City Hall floating across,
transfer to the 1 (oh, 1-California). Home.

Downtown, new town, a phoenix risen from 1906.
Water, milk, oil pour onto the flames, aftershocks, flashes
and I drink them down until my tongue is nothing

more than empty signifiers and massacres.
Born in the year of victim and verdugo,
I speak fluently a language adulterated with lead.

Psalm 144 (A New Mistranslation)

Verse 1:   *Blessed is the God who teaches my hands to fight and trains my fingers for war:*

Manufacturer's specifications: Spike's Tactical created a balanced reliable rifle that would bring an excellent fighting rifle to people of all abilities and resources. The every-man fighting rifle. We named it Crusader and engraved Psalm 144:1 on the lower receiver to hoist the flag of our faith and to make a statement, reminding our customers that we are with you. The war is here. We have a duty to defend our homeland and our way of life.

Verse 3:   God, what is man that you know him? What is a mortal that he enters your thoughts?

Washington Post: A spokesman for Spike's Tactical says—

Manufacturer's specifications: This rifle contains a selection of our finest components. This weapon balances the fine line between tactical and competition, light weight and dependability!

Manufacturer's specifications: With an unloaded weight of 6.65lbs and smooth shooting of a mid-length gas system, the Crusader is a versatile rifle at home or on the competition flat range as well as the two-way range.

Washington Post: —he initially floated the idea for the gun when he was asked during a company meeting about a year ago to name some technical specifications he'd like to see on a rifle. Without hesitation, Thomas, who had just come from listening to hours of unspecified news programming, blurted out an answer. 'I want

15

a rifle that no Muslim terrorist can use to murder innocent people,' he says. 'I half expected to be fired or at least not taken serious, but they took the ball and they ran with it.'

Verse 8: His mouth speaks falsehoods and his oaths and vows are lies.

Verse 9: God, I will sing a new song to you with my ten-stringed harp.

Manufacturer's specifications: And of course, each component is backed by the Spike's Tactical Lifetime Warranty.

Verse 11: Save me from the unknown, who speak falsehoods and raise their right hands to swear their lies.

Verse 12: Our sons are like saplings, grown from their youth and our daughters are like the stones hewn to build a shrine.

Verse 13: Our warehouses are full of produce of this kind and that, and many thousand cattle are in the fields.

Legal notice: This is a Title I Firearm. Title I firearms are ordinary rifles, pistols, revolvers, and shotguns. Title I firearms can be owned and built by any citizen who isn't considered to be a prohibited person by the Bureau of Alcohol, Tobacco, and Firearms.

reddit.com/r/ar15: Dude likes to larp as a Crusader a lot.

Meeting Three Ghosts in Belchite la Vieja

I meet George Orwell in Belchite la Vieja: surprising because he is dead, unsurprising because who else would haunt this place? The republican army took it, house by house, in the heat of an August like this one, committing atrocities for freedom. Failing. There is no water here. There was no water then. George Orwell is not thirsty. I am. I take out my iPhone and show him how to use the camera. I help him download a PDF of his own book. I play him a few tracks from a Florence and the Machine album. He likes the line about practical ghosts.

I meet Baron von Munchausen in Belchite la Vieja: he has been left behind by Terry Gilliam, who ran out of funding to bring home the star of his film. He doesn't mind because the next set sounds like a worse place to be stuck: same amount of no money and in *un lugar de La Mancha*, next to a NATO bombing range, *de cuyo nombre no me quiero acordar*. Baron von Munchausen likes Belchite la Vieja. He tells me that he spends time with Gustavo Adolfo and rides Bucéfalo around the perimeter at night. They fit through a hole in the chain-link fence, as long as nobody in the municipality fixes it. Robin Williams is here, too, spending eternity as an Italian pun. Baron von Muchausen can't stand it.

I meet King Alfonso I, called *Batallador*, in Belchite la Vieja: la very vieja, since he founded the city in the twelfth century. He has a hard time finding his way here since none of his buildings or fortifications has survived; the oldest is two-hundred years younger than he is and there's just one of that vintage. It has no roof and is held up by a wooden armature that confuses him. During the hour from noon to one he can follow the guides leading groups of tourists struggling to take photographs in the midday sun, but for twenty-three hours of most days, plus all of Sundays and holidays, he is alone and loses his way. I decide not to tell him about the new king and Belchite la Nueva.

Page Found Acephalous in the Venetian Ghetto

…the lagoon-streets
paved cosmopolitan
bring me past the *scuole*:
locked, unlit, too late,
but out of basilica shadows.
Plain white fronts, small windows:
houses of spite or self-preservation.
But I am no Jessica, convert,
shamed gombeen's daughter.
I ride gondolas short-wise
across the grand canal,
sailing against the law and the tide.

Some Day, Underwater Archaeologists

"Some day," he says, "underwater archaeologists
will write a doctoral dissertation
on the contents of my apartment."

The acqua alta spills out of the tops of his rain boots as he kneels
to get a closer look at a painting in the expatriated Fortuny museum.
I do not know it yet but I will never return.

I watched Jaws on my last flight here;
mid-air is the only congenial place to watch that movie.
I did not know that sharks had entered the Venetian lagoon.
I did not know there was a movie called *A Shark in Venice*.
Fewer sharks enter the lagoon
now that engineers have installed the half-functioning inflatable dam
     system
meant to protect the archipelago against the *acqua alta*
even though it turned out to deter sharks more effectively than floods.

(Julia Child would be jealous. The shark deterrent
she invented as an agent for the old OSS
was more effective against floods than sharks.)

Some day, I realize, underwater archaeologists
will find, upon necropsy, the artefacts of my brief presence
in the stomach of the last Great White that entered the lagoon:

An expired epi-pen
The weirdly-shaped ring my grandmother used to wear
Susan Orlean's book about the LA Public Library fire
The rest of my library, that might as well have burned
Most of an uneaten box of Altoids
The photographs that don't exist
The photographs I can't get off my old laptop
Shampoo and conditioner I thought I'd use in February
That little black dress with the bracket-shaped neckline

Two volumes of an Arabic-Italian dictionary set
The smallest jar of ground nutmeg

Hand-knit silk dress socks locked in a cupboard
The cupboard
Every blank notebook
One unopened bottle of *naranja* agria imported from the Americas

Some day, I know, underwater archaeologists
will revise their doctoral dissertation into a book
and exhibition catalogue. They will acknowledge

the veterinary pathologist
who necropsied the shark that consumed my brief presence
and carried it from the apartment out to the Adriatic Sea.

Alice in the Underworld

Alice, egyptcurious, found herself at the bottom of an undiscovered tomb shaft. She followed a desert hare that ran and disappeared, suggesting a mirage. There was plenty of use to her to read on the walls so she carried on as she did above ground. The wifi is surprisingly good in the pyramids; she could compose her books about Egypt and send out her manuscripts and no-one noticed she was missing, only reflecting later that her work gained a certain authenticity during this period. The dry air that keeps the mummies preserves work khakis, too, but she grew bored with her trousers and little by little opened the coffins and sarcophagi to replace her affected pith helmet with a golden headdress and her trousers with a once-white robe that she cinched at the waist so it fell like a flapper dress. She grabbed handfuls of faience scarabs and gold and refashioned them to drip from her ears and her neck. She hosted her own Egyptian revival tea party for one in the dark. But when she finally emerged with a perfect Cleopatra haircut, her readers grew inattentive and she longed for clothes like those in the tomb. Charles, egyptomaniac, seemed to rescue her, gave her new outfits. He made her image in his image, recalling her subterranean black in his silver. Each wished to believe the tomb had not aged her.

The hieroglyphic
(mad, white) rabbit signifies
to be, to exist.

Trying to Read the Radiology Report That Just Landed in My Inbox and I Am Not the Right Kind of Doctor for This

"I expressed to him my surprise at the findings and my dismay at the way I had received the results. I asked whether this had been sent to me by email because I am a physician and thus presumably more capable of understanding the information (which, it turns out, was a false assumption). 'Not at all,' he replied. 'It is mandatory that all patients receive biopsy results and lab values within 48 hours.'"

—Ellen M. Friedman, "You've Got Mail," Journal of the American Medical Association 315 (2016)

Scout radiograph of the pelvis is normal.

This is going to break your heart to read;
it's breaking my heart to write, but
don't come to see me tomorrow.
I've fallen in love with someone else
and even though she's not available
it's made me realize I'm not in love with you
(ma nonostante tutto ti voglio bene).

*The uterus is anteverted in orientation.
Fundus is in the midline.*

When M— broke things off with me
she did it by email, too, only more cruelly
than this, so I know you will be okay.
We had been together for ten years
and we have been together for one
so this can't be as bad as that was.
And I am less cruel.

*There are no Mullerian anomalies
or contour irregularities.*

I am about to fall in love
with the next woman of my life,

the woman of the rest of my life,
and you deserve to be the woman
of someone's life. I will never
have one woman of my life.
It's too late for me for that.

Contour defect located adjacent to the left cornu
measures 1.4 x .3 cm. Suspicious.

The right fallopian tube filled
to its proximal ampullary segment.

And besides, M— is letting
me see our daughter again.

Findings are in keeping with right tubal occlusion.
The left fallopian tube did not opacify.

I have my daughter back
and I don't need the hassle
of the Atlantic Ocean anymore,
of planning and passports and packing,
just to have a younger partner
so I can replace my child; but

Myometrial inversion was noted. Impression:
Occlusion of the bilateral fallopian tubes.

you're going to want kids
and I want to be with a woman
who has already raised her kids,
who is in her fifties,
who has no ambition left.

This could be further assessed
with sonogram as clinically indicated.

The Shark Is More Afraid, I Tell Myself

White liquid fog, *ex machina*:
metallic surroundings don't fade but disappear
as a shark brushes, reassuring, against my arm.
My breasts: point breaks for the sea
are cut away with scalpel and sharks' teeth,
reshaped and bound with cotton and ivy.

Next, but hours later, I kick the kelp
and tentacles wrapped around my feet.
A leech, a leak: dripping the salinity
that makes me, a small internal sea.
The shark is more afraid, I tell myself:
Mine is to survive, hers is to kill and revive me.

The Angel of Death Will Be Confused
(and Other Old Wives' Tales)
After Safia Elhillo

If you leave the toaster plugged in,
the house will burn down.

If you eat the heel of the bread,
you will bear boy-children.

If you name your child after a living relative,
the Angel of Death will be confused.

If you tell people you are Jewish—
there is no if; just don't.

If you laugh, the world laughs with you.
If you cry, you cry alone.

If you sprinkle Lourdes water,
it can't make things worse.

If you wear a hand of Fatima,
it will ward off bad luck.

If you wear many hands of Fatima,
you may need a stronger chain.

If you can't sleep,
put a lavender sachet under your pillow.

If you decide to have children,
be prepared to be on your own.

If you eat mushrooms,
you won't get cancer.

If I eat mushrooms, maybe
the cancer will go into remission

until
western medicine has time to find a cure.

If a sick person changes their name,
the Angel of Death will be confused.

If I die, promise you'll take care of yourself:
find a yoga instructor, go to the allergist.

First Day Past the World to Come

Nel mezzo del cammin di nostra vita—and I hope I think of something better to shout than "what the hell?!" when I pass through the archway that tells *voi ch'intrate* to *lasciare ogni speranza*. I want to meet Filippo Argenti and find out what he did to Dante to get here. Nobody knows. I think Virgil will let me if I ask; he let Dante sit with Brunetto Latini. I want to meet Geryone because I liked the sculpture I saw of his feet in the Metropolitan Museum. If my Brunetta were here I'd choose to sit with her instead of gawping at Geryone. Maybe she is. Maybe she'd have more fun here. I never got around to reading the *Paradiso*. Bob Dylan is here, too, same reason as me. It's a surprise because we're both left out of the book. At least now I know which poet was tangled up in blue.

I'm Not Russian

but my grandmother's samovar is on my sideboard.
but other people's Russian grandmothers approach me on the street.
but their Russian grandmothers think I am and insist.
   In Russian.
but I've learned to say *ya ne-pnemayu* to protest. It doesn't help.
and nobody believes me.

Couplet with 'Ode to Walt Whitman'
Ars Poetica after Federico García Lorca

I. The retired English teacher in my poetry class

who thinks that Walt Whitman is the beginning and the end of
American poetry and that he himself was a hero for selling paperback
copies of *Frankenstein* to his public high school students at cost and
that Walt Whitman was the beginning and the end of American
poetry and that a whitewashed reference to MLK and the Black boys
who were a part of the landscape he knew growing up in Brooklyn
makes his work searching and antiracist and that women write about
sex and say *fuck* just because we can but there's no artistic value when
we do it because Walt Whitman, who was the beginning and the end
of American poetry, already innovated writing about sex and that was
powerful and prophetic and all of that—

and all of that

reminds me why I thought I hated literature when I was in high school.
That's not Walt Whitman's fault. It's Lorca's fault, for opening Whitman's
tomb and dragging his corpse back to New York City and leaving it on
the banks of the Hudson River where English teachers could find it;
and it's my fault, ours, for not keeping vigil.

II. A girl poet does not have to justify her use of these words:

bitch, vagina, cunnilingus, the Ottoman Empire, hemlock, fucking,
cojonudo (sounds worse than it is), *cabrón* (is only a funny word inside
my own head), ass-trumpet, twerking, snail-jousting, abbess, frog, toad,
cock, buck, bull, branches, basket, booty, green, green, green, scissors,
ruler, contest, Eileen Myles' pronouns (they/them), quarter, abscess,
fly, fascist, *gnudi*, Portia, *The Penguin Book of Erotic Stories by Women*
(although good luck with that, because it doesn't scan), Benedict
Cumberbatch (double dactyl), Walt Whitman, Federico García Lorca,
Balthazar, Venus, nickled-and-dimed, Mr. Jack Spicer, President James
Madison, closed, open, closed, fuck, fucked, and mercy.

This Book
Ars Poetica after Yolanda Wisher

I tell myself: No more literature poems.
No more rewriting others' good poem-poems,
No more me overthinking-poems,
Or leave our lagoon world sinking-poems, but
More five years with my shrink(ing)-poems.
Readers, trying nice, say: You do you-poems, and
Maybe this is the truth-poems:
Nothing exists but the fruit of before you-poems.

S.J. Pearce is a writer and translator who lives in New York City. A scholar of medieval poetry and translation, she came to the practice of poetry during the COVID-19 pandemic. A member of the 2022 Brooklyn Poets Mentorship Program cohort.

Her poetry and translations have appeared in *The Laurel Review, Asymptote, Copihue, Couplet Poetry, River Heron Review* and others; her public-facing literary criticism has appeared in the *LA Review of Books, Public Books* and the *Washington Post.*

Incident Names is her first collection of poetry and was a finalist for chapbook competitions held by *The Laurel Review* and Omnidawn Press and was long listed in the chapbook competition held by Verse/Tomaz Salamun Foundation.

An associate professor at New York University, her first academic monograph, *The Andalusi Literary and Intellectual Tradition* (Bloomington, 2017) was the recipient of the 2019 La Corónica International Book Prize and her current work explores the repurposing of medieval poetry for modern nationalist interests.